Online Rights and Responsibilities

Digital Citizenship

Sloane Gould

COMPUTER KIDS
Powered by Computational Thinking

PowerKiDS
press.

Published in 2018 by The Rosen Publishing Group, Inc.
29 East 21st Street, New York, NY 10010

Book Design: Jennifer Ryder-Talbot
Editor: Caitie McAneney

Photo Credits: Cover, p. 5 Syda Productions/Shutterstock.com; p. 6, 12 Dragon
Images/Shutterstock.com; p. 8 Shestakoff/Shutterstock.com; p. 10-11 lightwavemedia/
Shutterstock.com; p. 14 India Picture/Shutterstock.com; p. 17 Prostock-studio/
Shutterstock.com; p. 18-19 Sabphoto/Shutterstock.com; p. 20 Burdun Iliya/
Shutterstock.com.

Library of Congress Cataloging-in-Publication Data

Names: Gould, Sloane.
Title: Online rights and responsibilities: digital citizenship / Sloane Gould.
Description: New York : Rosen Classroom, 2018. | Series: Computer Kids: Powered by
Computational Thinking | Includes glossary and index.
Identifiers: LCCN ISBN 9781538353035 (pbk.) | ISBN 9781538324202 (library bound) |
ISBN 9781538355633 (6 pack) | ISBN 9781538352687 (ebook)
Subjects: LCSH: Online etiquette--Juvenile literature. | Internet--Moral and ethical aspects
-Juvenile literature. | Internet--Safety measures--Juvenile literature.
Classification: LCC TK5105.878 G68 2018 | DDC 303.48'33--dc23

Manufactured in the United States of America

CPSIA Compliance Information: Batch #WS18RC: For Further Information contact Rosen Publishing, New York, New York at 1-800-237-9932

Table of Contents

Using the Internet

The Internet is one of your most useful tools. With a few clicks, it can connect you with almost anyone in the world. You can learn information about any subject, from dinosaurs to ancient peoples to how a bill becomes a law. You can **download** music, games, books, and videos. You can express yourself by posting things that you've created. You can use it at home and at school.

How do you use the Internet? Have you had positive experiences online? Have you had negative experiences? It's important to remember that you have rights when you're using the Internet. You also have a responsibility to act appropriately. Learning your rights and responsibilities can help you get the most out of your online experience!

Everyone should learn about their online rights and responsibilities, no matter their age!

You Have Rights!

Have you ever studied the Bill of Rights in school? This part of the U.S. Constitution **guarantees** rights to all citizens. People have the right to free speech, the right to practice any religion, and the right to a free press, among other rights. These guaranteed rights protect citizens.

It's important to know your rights as a U.S. citizen and digital citizen!

You have rights online, too. You have the right to express yourself in any way that is respectful and true. For example, if you want to start a blog, you can write about your ideas and thoughts, as long as they don't hurt anyone. You can record yourself singing or post poems that you wrote to an online **platform**. You can read news and articles online because of the freedom of press.

U.S. Bill of Rights

freedom of speech

freedom of religion

freedom of press

freedom to assemble

right to a fair trial

People may try to post hurtful things about you online. You have the right to report them to the website's **administrators**.

8

Reporting Harassment

You have the right to be safe at home, in school, in public places, and online. If you are ever **harassed** online in any way, you should tell a parent or other trusted adult. In some **extreme** cases, the police may even get involved.

What does online harassment look like? Sometimes people **threaten** others online, saying they will physically hurt them or ruin their **reputation**. People may call others very hurtful names and make repeated hurtful remarks against them. Sometimes people harass others for a long period of time. You should always report harassment. You have the right to a safe experience online.

Staying Safe

Many times, people are harassed online by people they already know in person. However, strangers might bother you online, too. If a stranger is older than you, they should never contact you. You have the right to report this person for your own safety.

Talk to your parents if you ever feel unsafe online.

Never talk to people you don't know online. You never know a person's true identity. Even if someone says they know your parents or says they are your age, you can't tell for sure. It is best to tell a parent or trusted adult if you are ever approached by a stranger online. They can tell you how to stay safe. If the stranger won't leave you alone or says inappropriate things, then they should be reported to the police.

Right to Privacy

You have a right to privacy online. It is a crime to look at or use someone else's private computer account, unless you are given permission. It is also a crime to **intercept** someone's private emails or messages online. Even if you accidentally leave a private account open in school, people should never use it.

You can protect yourself from an invasion of privacy by always signing out of accounts in public places. Also, you can change your privacy settings on social media accounts to control what people can see. Make sure to make your password very strong, so no one can break into your accounts.

A strong password uses a combination of letters, words, and symbols that is hard to guess.

You can keep your information private by not sharing personal information online. Never tell someone your full name, address, or phone number.

Before you post something online, ask yourself these
questions: Is it true? Is it helpful? Is it respectful?

Online Identity

You have rights to express yourself, be safe, and keep your accounts private. These are meant to protect you when you are navigating the online world. You also have responsibilities when you are using the Internet.

It's important to understand that as you post or **interact** with people online, you are creating an online identity or digital identity. Do you have a social media account? If so, you need to think about how you are presenting yourself to the world. Are you kind, helpful, and appropriate? Do you say things that are true and respectful? Good digital citizens present themselves in this way. It's important to keep your interactions online positive and present yourself in the best way possible.

No Stealing

You wouldn't take a book or movie from a store without paying for it, would you? That would be stealing and it is against the law. However, many people steal content, movies, and music online. They illegally download and **distribute** work that was made by other people, without paying or giving credit to that person.

You have the responsibility to follow **copyright** law. Give credit where credit is due. If you want to use another person's writing in your work, you must credit that person correctly. You must also do this for artwork, videos, and music. If you want to download music or movies, make sure to do it in a legal way. That often means paying for the songs or movies.

Have you ever downloaded music online?
How can you do it legally?

No Hacking

Just as you have a right to privacy online, other people also have a right to privacy. That means you have a responsibility to respect other people's privacy. Imagine you go to the school library and realize that your classmate hasn't logged out of their social media account. It might seem funny to search around their account or post something on it. However, using a computer or account without authorization, or permission, is wrong.

Some people learn how to hack into other people's accounts or computers. That means they enter them without authorization. Even if you have the ability to do something like this, you must remain a good digital citizen and leave other people's accounts alone.

It's important to report hacking if you see it happening.

Cyberbullying often happens behind closed doors. It's important to talk with a parent or teacher about it if you see it happening.

No Cyberbullying

Cyberbullying is bullying online. In person, someone might push, hit, or say mean things to a person. Online, people who bully others are given new tools to cause harm. They might harass a person, post hurtful comments or pictures of a person, or tell lies about a person.

You have the responsibility to act with respect online. That means no cyberbullying. If you see someone cyberbullying another person, you can report them to the website's administrators or to another helpful adult, such as a teacher or parent. If you know someone who is being cyberbullied, you can stand up for them and show your support for them. You can help make the Internet a friendlier place!

A Community of Users

The Internet is a community of users from around the world. Each one has a right to have a positive experience online. Each user also has the responsibility to keep the Internet safe for others.

When you act appropriately and respectfully online, you are being a good digital citizen. You should think before you post something. Make sure what you say won't harm others unfairly. You can report people for inappropriate actions or hurtful remarks. Most importantly, you should keep yourself safe online by making strong passwords, making strong privacy settings, and never talking to strangers. It's important to learn about federal laws for Internet use. Knowing your rights and responsibilities keeps you and others safe and happy online!

Glossary

administrator: One who manages a website, business, or school.

copyright: The legal right to copy, publish, sell, or distribute the matter and form of something.

distribute: To give out or deliver something.

download: To move or copy something such as a file or program from the Internet to a computer or device.

extreme: Great or severe.

guarantee: To assure the fulfillment of a condition.

harass: To annoy or threaten persistently.

interact: To act on one another.

intercept: To interrupt communication.

platform: A place or opportunity for public discussion.

reputation: The views that are held about something or someone.

threaten: To warn someone about an intent to harm them.

Index